RAILWAY MOODS

THE FFESTINIOG RAILWAY

CLIFF THOMAS

HALSGROVE

First published in Great Britain in 2007

Title page: *Prince* hauls a train of historic FR 'bug box'
four-wheel coaches away from Porthmadog Harbour station.

British Library Cataloguing-in-Publication Data
A CIP record for this title is available from the British Library

ISBN 978 1 84114 600 3

HALSGROVE
Halsgrove House,
Ryelands Farm Industrial Estate,
Bagley Green, Wellington, Somerset TA21 9PZ
Tel: 01823 653777 Fax: 01823 216796
email: sales@halsgrove.com
website: www.halsgrove.com

Printed and bound by D'Auria Industrie Grafiche, Italy

INTRODUCTION

The 1ft 11½ins gauge Ffestiniog Railway is the oldest unamalgamated railway company in the world and the first narrow gauge line in Britain authorised to carry passengers.

In 1811 William Maddocks' mile-long embankment (The Cob) was completed across the River Glaslyn estuary and by the 1820s Port Madoc harbour was completed at the western end, leading to the idea of building a railway to connect the slate quarries at Blaenau Ffestiniog with the sea. The Act of Parliament incorporating the Festiniog Railway Company (incorrectly spelt with a single 'F') was passed on 23 May 1832, construction started in 1833 and it opened on 20 April 1836.

Slate was transported from the Blaenau quarries downwards by gravity over nearly 14 miles of line engineered to an almost continuous gradient, save the use of two inclines. Horses pulled empty wagons back up from the Harbour wharves. The inclines were eliminated when the Moelwyn tunnel was opened in 1842, with the Garnedd tunnel following in 1851 – their narrow bores account for the tight FR loading gauge.

The first locomotives were delivered from George England & Co in July 1863 leading to the introduction of passenger services, the first official passenger train running on 5 January 1865. Plans to double the track were dropped following the arrival of the revolutionary double-ended loco *Little Wonder* in 1869. The first narrow gauge locomotive built to Robert Fairlie's patent, it provided a powerful loco which could negotiate sharp curves due to its pair of short wheelbase bogies. It brought the FR national and international fame and the type became synonymous with the Ffestiniog.

In January 1873, the first iron-framed bogie passenger carriages to be built in Britain for any gauge – and the first bogie passenger carriages in the world to be built for a narrow gauge line – were delivered.

The Ffestiniog Railway is famed for its double ended Fairlie locomotives.
This study is of *David Lloyd George*, built new by the FR at Boston Lodge and
pictured here at Harbour station three years after its 1992 introduction to traffic.

In 1923 a link was built between the FR and the Welsh Highland Railway in Porthmadog. The WHR's 22-mile line to Dinas closed in 1933, following which the FR leased it until 1936. The FR ceased to operate on 1 August 1946. Preservation proposals dating from 1951 led to The Ffestiniog Railway Preservation Society being incorporated as the Ffestiniog Railway Society Ltd on 24 December 1954. Meanwhile, a group led by Alan Peglar gained a majority shareholding in the FR company on 24 June 1954, this controlling interest being passed to the Ffestiniog Railway Trust.

Public services across The Cob commenced on 23 July 1955, extending to Minffordd from 19 May 1956, Penrhyn from 20 April 1957 and Tan-y-Bwlch from 5 April 1958. Double Fairlie *Taliesin* (named *Livingston Thompson* until 1932) returned to service in 1957.

An electricity generating scheme which flooded the track north of the Moelwyn tunnel brought years of legal wrangling. Work to by-pass the new reservoir started in January 1965. Passenger trains returned to Dduallt on 6 April 1968, by which time work on a deviation to gain height from Dduallt was proceeding – involving building the only spiral track in Britain. A new Moelwyn tunnel was bored and the first revenue-earning train ran through to Llyn Ystradau (the new lake) on 8 July 1977.

A new Tanygrisau station was opened on 24 June 1978 and the final mile and a half of track to Blaenau was made continuous on 24 May 1981. A new joint station with BR was built at Blaenau, becoming fully operational in 1982. New locomotives – including Double and Single Fairlie types – and carriages have been constructed and historic stock restored.

The FR is now rebuilding the Welsh Highland Railway. With the WHR open between Caernarfon and Rhyd Ddu, work is forging ahead on the remainder of the line, which will once again link with the FR at Harbour station in Porthmadog.

MAP OF THE AREA

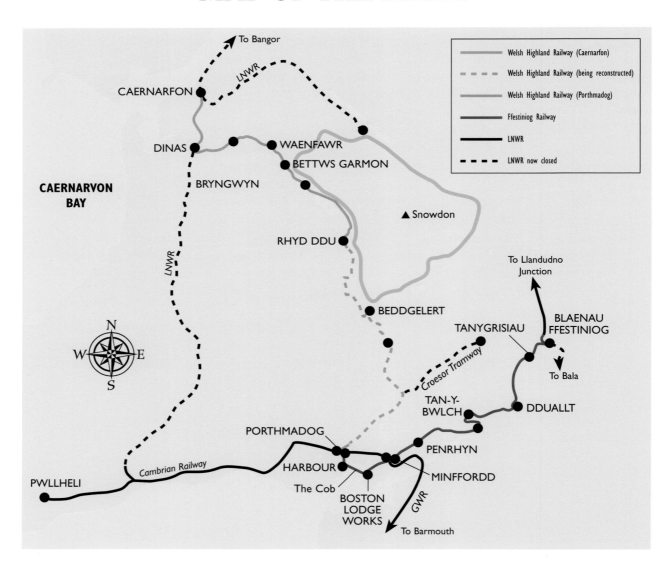

To Bangor

LNWR

CAERNARFON

DINAS

WAENFAWR

BETTWS GARMON

BRYNGWYN

CAERNARVON BAY

LNWR

▲ Snowdon

RHYD DDU

To Llandudno Junction

BEDDGELERT

TANYGRISIAU

BLAENAU FFESTINIOG

To Bala

Croesor Tramway

TAN-Y-BWLCH

DDUALLT

N
W E
S

PORTHMADOG

PENRHYN

Cambrian Railway

HARBOUR

MINFFORDD

The Cob

PWLLHELI

BOSTON LODGE WORKS

GWR

To Barmouth

	Welsh Highland Railway (Caernarfon)
	Welsh Highland Railway (being reconstructed)
	Welsh Highland Railway (Porthmadog)
	Ffestiniog Railway
	LNWR
	LNWR now closed

The turnouts at Harbour station are operated by traditional levers in a ground frame. In the background, *David Lloyd George* prepares to depart with a train for Blaenau.

A few minutes after the previous picture was taken, *David Lloyd George* steams away from the station. Although the bunkers on top of the water tanks contain coal this is an illusion, the loco being an oil burner at the time.

Blanche was an 0-4-0ST when built by Hunslet in 1893 to work for the Penrhyn quarry operation. After acquisition by the FR in December 1963 she was equipped with a leading pony truck and a tender.

Linda is a sister of *Blanche*, also built as an 0-4-0ST by Hunslet in 1893 for Penrhyn.
She first came to the FR in July 1962 and has been fitted with a pony truck and tender.

Earl of Merioneth makes a quite spectacular departure from Harbour station.
This Double-Fairlie, built by the FR at Boston Lodge in 1979, had a rather utilitarian design
of side tanks and provided the FR with an effective rather than attractive locomotive.

The considerably more traditional appearance given to 1992-built *David Lloyd George* compared with the functional late 1970s construction of *Earl of Merioneth* is very clear when compared with the previous picture.

This interesting line-up of locomotives, comprising (left to right) *Palmerston, Taliesin, Prince* and *David Lloyd George* was photographed at the FR's October 2002 Vintage Gala.

Following the 12 October 2002 line-up pictured on the previous page, *Prince* pulls away from Harbour with a demonstration train comprising vintage freight stock and slate wagons.

The spring bulbs are flowering in this 29 April 2005 picture of American-built
1918-vintage 2-4-0 diesel *Moelwyn* at Harbour station.

This loco is a B-Class 0-4-0ST originally built to work on the Darjeeling Himalayan Railway. Later sold to the USA and subsequently purchased and brought back to Britain by Adrian Shooter to work on his private railway, the first time it had been steamed in public outside India was during its visit to the FR's 29 April-2 May 2005 gala which celebrated the Golden Jubilee of the railway's revival.
The two coaches are replica DHR vehicles, constructed by the FR at Boston Lodge for Mr Shooter.

Trains leaving Harbour station round a significant curve from the platform on to the Cob, hence it is the fireman who leans out of the cab of *David Lloyd George* to ensure that the train is intact as the journey to Blaenau commences.

The mile-long Cob immediately opens up magnificent views for passengers with the sea to the right and the mountains of Snowdonia to the left. Here, the two 'FR Ladies' *Blanche* and *Linda* gently approach Harbour station on 8 October 2000.

This 30 April 2005 arrival is headed by *Earl of Merioneth* and 1917-built
Alco 2-6-2T *Mountaineer*. The name applied to the latter was carried
by one of the FR's original George England-built locomotives.

The nature of the Cob becomes clear in this view, the small size of the 0-6-0 diesel *Criccieth Castle* hauling three four-wheel carriages accentuating the scale of achievement in its construction in the early 1800s.

Taliesin is returning to Harbour station with a rake of vintage carriages in this May 2004 view of the Cob. The buildings in the foreground are apartments constructed on what were once loading wharfs where slate was transhipped from FR wagons to sea-going sailing ships.

The steam from *Prince's* whistle seems to be blending with the clouds as the 1863-vintage loco reaches the far end of the Cob with a demonstration train of vintage freight wagons. At the time of this 5 May 2002 picture *Prince* was an oil-burner, hence virtually no exhaust emanates from the chimney.

Palmerston, like *Prince*, is an original George England-built FR loco dating from 1863. However, *Palmerston* burns coal in its firebox, providing a more traditional locomotive exhaust as it reaches the end of the Cob quite late in the afternoon on 12 October 2002.

At the end of the Cob the line swings left around the front of Boston Lodge Works, as shown by this 5 May 2003 picture of *Prince* returning to Porthmadog.

Kerr Stewart 0-4-2ST *Stanhope*, part of the Moseley Railway Trust collection, visited the FR in May 2003 for an 'Interactive Gala'. In essence, people pay to fulfil their railway ambitions at these events, ranging from working with a guard to riding on a loco footplate.

Over the years, photography at Boston Lodge has included being frozen by winds off the sea and soaked by driving rain, but 3 May 1998 was one of those glorious occasions which make other memories fade away. Hunslet 0-4-0ST *Lilla* poses with restored wagons with the mountains of Snowdonia as the perfect backdrop.

Linda, returning to Porthmadog, is pictured on the section between Boston Lodge works and Boston Lodge halt, which lies just beyond the old loco shed on the left of the frame.

I am not a fan of faces on locomotives, but could not help being amused by this picture. The eyes on the diesel seem to convey a sense of anxiety over the degree of effort being expended by the steam loco, *Blanche*, pushing it along from behind as the unusual pairing heads rapidly towards Rhiw Plas bridge on the way to Minffordd!

Minffordd is the first passing place on the single line and *Earl of Merioneth* has received clearance to continue down to Harbour station. A new set of tanks have been constructed for this loco and will be fitted when the time arrives for its next overhaul. These will considerably alter, for the better, the appearance of this Double-Fairlie.

Taliesin has arrived at Minffordd with a 'Talking Train' working on 1 May 2004. This new service offers a more leisurely trip up the line than does a normal train, with each passenger being given a handset which conveys a commentary and much information about features surrounding the railway.

Opposite: At Minffordd, the FR meets the national railway network. Today, a Cambrian Coast line station remains, but in the past the yard was an important interchange location where slate from Blaenau was transferred from FR wagons to the standard gauge. The yard is often used during FR gala events, when shuttle trains are run from the FR station. This example is being worked top-and-tail by vintage FR internal combustion locomotives, that nearest the camera being Simplex *Mary Ann*; at the far end is *Moelwyn*.

Minffordd yard is principally the FR permanent way depot, but the extensive trackwork is ideal for presenting shunting demonstrations employing the smaller locomotives during special events. Here, FR resident *Lilla* is dropping down in to the main yard while *Palmerston* pauses for a moment in the background.

In this 8 October 2000 picture *Palmerston* is displaying no shortage
of steam while it energetically shunts slate wagons around the yard.

The 8 October 2000 'Slate Shunt' demonstration involved a complex series of choreographed moves by several locos, the sequence ending in a grand finale at a rail crossing in the yard where the whistles were blown on a cue from the signalman controlling the operation. The locos are (left to right) *Gwynedd*, *Palmerston*, *Lilla* and *Cloister* (the first and last being visiting locos) – and the smokebox of *Palmerston* was not fitted with a propeller during the event, it is the fan of an old engine in one of the wagons!

The Slate Shunt concept originated with the idea of offering special footplate experience courses using *Lilla* to shunt slate wagons around. This has raised considerable amounts of cash to fund special projects. It has also presented the opportunity to show small locomotives working at the kind of job they were originally built for.

The FR's 29 April-2 May 2005 celebration of the Golden Jubilee of its revival featured
a 'Turtle Ffest' in Minffordd yard. 'Turtle' is a nickname applied to First World War
vintage Motor Rail 'Protected' Simplex locomotives. Some have likened these to being
like small tanks on railway wheels. Perhaps this picture of the Moseley Railway
Trust's WDLR No. 3090 and the National Railway Museum's WDLR No. 3098,
which is cared for by the Leighton Buzzard Railway, suggests they have a point!

This privately-owned steam-powered monorail locomotive visited the FR's
April/May 2005 gala and ran on a specially set up length of track in Minffordd yard.

Returning to Minffordd station, *Taliesin* waits in the platform for *Linda*
to cross with her Porthmadog-bound service on 1 May 2004.

The crew of *Taliesin* take possession of the staff which gives them authority to leave Minffordd and proceed on to the single line to Porthmadog. The waiting shelter, a replica of the original, had only recently been completed when this 5 May 2002 picture was taken.

Blanche, actually at the head of a demonstration mineral train rather than a passenger service in this 8 October 2000 picture, prepares to continue up the line away from Minffordd station.

The diesel tractor *Moelwyn* and the small bogie brake coach No. 10
are caught in the sun at Minffordd on 5 May 2002.

Under a rather threatening sky, *David Lloyd George* and *Prince* make an evocatively steamy departure from Minffordd on 8 October 2000.

Opposite:
It has become traditional for small visiting locomotives to make a special trip up the full line to Blaenau, sometimes in the morning, more often in the evening, when the route is clear of normal service trains. The conditions appear quite pleasant as Hunslet 0-4-0STs *Alice* and *Velinheli* take water at Minffordd on 6 May 1997. The writer can vouch that it was very cold by the time this trip reached Blaenau – and he was in a brake van compartment, not sitting in an open wagon as were some hardy souls!

After leaving Minffordd, the line runs up Gwyndy Bank en route to Penrhyn.
Linda is pictured on the bank in the unusual situation of not being attached to a train.
The occasion was 2 May 1999 when, as part of a cavalcade of locos through Minffordd
station during the 1-3 May Railffest99 event, the locos were taken up on to the bank
to wait for their turn to run down in front of the gathered crowds.

Also awaiting his turn on Gwyndy Bank on 2 May 1999 is *Prince*, as a van demonstrates that the loading gauge for bridges over lanes is as confined as that for locos working on the FR. The Grand Locomotive Cavalcade actually involved 19 items of motive power.

At Penrhyn, immediately after the train leaves the station the line crosses a road on the level. In this 25 October 1996 picture, visiting Hunslet 0-4-0STs *Lilian* and *George Sholto* are about to cross the road on their way down from Blaenau. The open wagon is typical passenger accommodation for these special runs by visiting locos!

The sky was beginning to look a little threatening as *Earl of Merioneth* approaches Penrhyn crossing in this 6 May 1997 view.

Above Penrhyn there is a passing loop and signal cabin at Rhiw Goch, although this is not a station. The driver of *Linda* is approaching the signal cabin while the author's wife, Carrie, takes stock for a moment from the seat in the loco's tender.

Having crossed an elegant bridge high over the road, *Linda* runs in to Tan-y-Bwlch station on 1 May 2004.

The tracks of Tan-y-Bwlch station describe a gentle 'S' shape as can be seen from the footbridge in this 12 October 2002 view. The up passenger train waits in the platform while its passengers are enthralled by the 25-wagon gravity slate train which is rushing through the station. The crews are riding the wagons just as used to occur when the FR was built, although in those days the gravity trains were much longer – and handled by rather fewer brakesmen than is the case nowadays!

Tan-y-Bwlch is not only a passing place, but a water stop for the ascending locos. The large tank has two outlet pipes – very handy for double-headed trains! Of special interest in this picture of *Linda* beside the tank on 25 October 1996 is that she does not have the tender which she normally runs with, and which contains the fuel for her oil burners. Moreover, she has a backsheet to the cab in contrast to other pictures in this book which show her with an open-backed cab. Her original cab sheet was fitted for a brief period to restore her Penrhyn appearance, while the oil tank has been concealed in the leading wagon. It was impractical to remove her leading pony truck to fully present her 2-4-0ST Penrhyn configuration however!

While the FR has paid staff, volunteers are the lifeblood of the railway. Paul Lewin, General Manager of the FR, was a long-time locomotive volunteer (he appears on the footplate of *Velinheli* in the picture on page 43) before his appointment to the top job – and he keeps his hand in as a volunteer driver, being at the regulator of *Taliesin* in this 1 May 2004 picture.

The crew of *David Lloyd George* in this pair
of pictures were also both volunteers.
As the fireman refills the tanks with water
(right) the driver oils round the motion (above)
before the loco continues its journey.

Single-Fairlie *Taliesin* shunts vintage carriage stock in Tan-y-Bwlch station on 2 June 2002. The semaphore signal in the background is a replica of the original and is not employed for present day FR operations.

This view, taken from the footplate of *David Lloyd George*, shows that our colour light signal is showing a red aspect as we wait beside the water tower at Tan-y-Bwlch for *Merddin Emrys* to enter the station with a train from Blaenau.

Cleared to leave the loop at Tan-y-Bwlch, *Linda* draws
forward on to the single line to continue towards Blaenau.

As it was being revived, if it were to return to Blaenau the FR had to resolve the problem of the trackbed being flooded by a pumped storage scheme reservoir near Tan-y-Grisau. To gain height, a spiral track was constructed at Dduallt. *Linda* is pictured on 23 October 1996 part-way round the line which turns a complete circle as part of this 'deviation'.

Having gained height on the spiral at Dduallt the line runs through a new Moelwyn tunnel, emerges above the reservoir and crosses two minor roads to reach Tan-y-Grisiau. Crossing one of these roads, this unusual triple-header is a down train pictured on 3 May 1999. Nearest the camera is *Earl of Merioneth* (which had spent the day at Glan-y-Pwll offering 'drive a Double-Fairlie' opportunities) which had been attached to the locos which had taken the train up, *Mountaineer* (middle) and *Linda*.

Taken a little further round towards Tan-y-Grisiau (the station is not far out of the frame to the right) *Linda* and *Blanche* skirt round behind the café and generating station visitor centre opposite the reservoir on their way down to Porthmadog.

Linda is pictured on 1 June 2002 as she enters Tan-y-Grisau station just after crossing a tumbling river.

At the Blaenau end of Tan-y-Grisau station, the line becomes quite intimate with the cottages of the village. *David Lloyd George* is pictured on 12 October 2002 during an FR Vintage Gala.

Prince leaves Tan-y-Grisau station and heads for Blaenau with a train of empty slate wagons. Such a working recalls the very reason why steam was introduced to the FR. Originally, slate came down by gravity and the wagons were hauled back up by horses. The introduction of steam enabled the empty wagons to be returned to the quarries by locomotives instead of horses – and *Prince* was one of those early locomotives, albeit looking somewhat different from its present day appearance.

This view of *David Lloyd George* with a down working of freight wagons
is taken from the Blaenau end of the Tan-y-Grisau station platform.

This view from above the line shows a down train from Blaenau approaching Tan-y-Grisau station, the curved platform of which can be made out on the upper left side of the frame.

Linda and *Blanche* seem almost to be skimming along the roof tops as they make their way past Tan-y-Grisau in this 12 October 2002 picture.

In reality, the line clings to the side of the mountain by virtue of a huge stone wall.
This picture of *David Lloyd George* heading a down train was taken on 28 October 1997.

This rather different angle of *David Lloyd George* on the front of a down service emphasises the impressive mountain scenery at the top end of the railway.

From a photographic viewpoint, one might argue that a Double-Fairlie is the ideal locomotive – you get a smokebox-first shot regardless of which direction the loco is travelling! *David Lloyd George*, working a Porthmadog-bound train, is approaching the houses of Tan-y-Grisau in this 1 June 2002 picture.

On the other hand, the open backed cab of *Linda* offers an interesting view of the footplate crew as she runs through the same location as the previous view a little later in the day.

Linda has left Tan-y-Grisau behind and hurries on towards Glan-y-Pwll.

Journey's end has been reached, *Linda* being pictured in the loop at Blaenau Ffestiniog as, having run round the train, she edges up to the carriages to couple up ready for the return trip.

Earl of Merioneth, carrying the same headboard as it had two decades before, hauls a celebratory special into Blaenau Ffestiniog station on1 June 2002, re-enacting the train run in 1982 when the FR returned to the town.

Blaenau Ffestiniog station lies in a town surrounded by mountains and huge tips of slate waste generated from the quarries. The island platform at the bottom of the steps is used by the Ffestiniog Railway, while to the right are the standard gauge tracks of the Conwy Valley line.

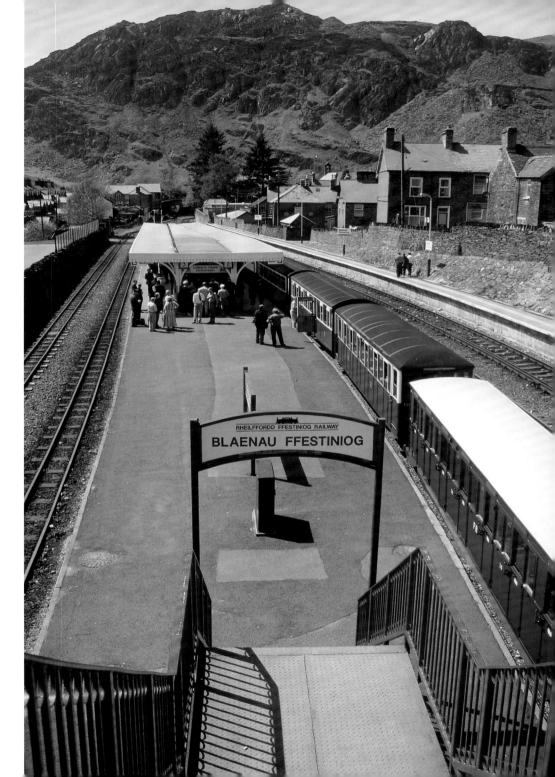

There is always a special atmosphere when photographing steam locomotives at night. Such was the case when FR locos were posed at Boston Lodge on 25 October 1997. This is *David Lloyd George*.

Palmerston also took a turn over the loco pit in the yard.

Next to be placed over the servicing pit, in which lights had been placed to supplement the more conventional lighting, was *Prince*.

A different position enabled the lights of Boston Lodge works
to be shown behind *David Lloyd George*.

Lilla also had her turn under the floodlighting during the October 1997 session. The temperature when the shoot was complete was about what one may anticipate at night, in October, beside the sea!

In case anyone has ever doubted tales of loco crews cooking on the shovel in the firebox of their steeds, this should confirm the stories are true. The driver of *Britomart* cooked sausages and bacon for his lunchtime rolls on this occasion. Of course, this only works with coal fired locos, and most of the FR fleet have been oil fired for many years. Several locos, however, are being converted to coal firing in view of the rising cost of oil.

LOCOMOTIVES

Around the 1940s *Palmerston* had been reduced to the status of being a static boiler providing steam to power a hammer in the Smith's shop at Boston Lodge. Fortunately the loco survived and has been restored to provide us with this splendid sight.

Lilla was built in 1891 for the Cilgwyn Quarry, was sold to the Penrhyn Quarry in May 1928 and was bought privately for preservation in 1963. In 1997 she was purchased via the Festiniog Railway Trust and the FR became her home.

Linda, pictured running past Boston Lodge, originally worked at Penrhyn quarry and is named after a member of the quarry owner's family. She has run in a Penrhyn livery for some years.

NGG16 Garratt No. 138 was acquired from South Africa to work on the revived Welsh Highland Railway. The FR had to undertake extensive preparatory work before the loco could fulfil this role. Although far too large to work on the FR main line, it has worked on Ffestiniog metals. This picture was taken on 5 April 1997 as it was run up and down about 400 yards of siding beside the river at Glan-y-Pwll and the author even had a brief turn at the regulator. The rain, falling when this picture was taken, turned to sleet by the end of the day!

Double-Fairlie *Livingston Thompson* was withdrawn from service in 1971 and for many years has been exhibited in the National Railway Museum in York. It was moved out of the NRM to join the 2005 celebration of the 50th anniversary of the preservation of the FR and is pictured at Harbour station – as a static exhibit – on 30 April 2005. It has since returned to the NRM.

Double-Fairlie *Merddin Emrys* also appeared at Harbour station for the FR's 2005 celebrations following an extensive overhaul. The work included constructing new tanks over a Christmas 2003 blitz by volunteers which hugely improve the loco's appearance, further enhanced by cladding which gives the illusion that *Merddin* has a wagon-top boiler. The loco had steamed itself over the Cob to appear in this 30 April 2005 picture, although examination would show that there had not been time to add the motion to the Port end bogie; *Merddin Emrys* was, therefore, actually working as a Single Fairlie! The post-overhaul black paint is not unusual for an FR loco, the full livery was subsequently applied after a period of running-in.

The Saturday evening of 30 April 2005 at Harbour saw a long-anticipated line-up of five Fairlie locomotives. Long shadows and the sun in the west made for awkward photographic conditions – fortunately Double-Fairlies can be shot smokebox first from either direction, but little could be done about *Taliesin*! Left to right are: *Earl of Merioneth*, *David Lloyd George*, Single-Fairlie *Taliesin*, *Livingston Thompson* and *Merddin Emrys*.

Could one ask for a more attractive scene as 0-4-0STT *Prince* poses in the sun at Harbour station on 1 May 2005 with a quarryman's coach and a rake of 'bug box' four-wheel coaches?

BOSTON LODGE

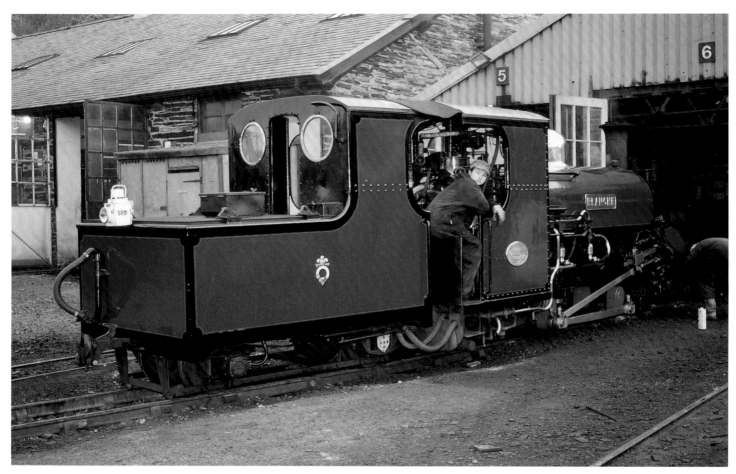

Boston Lodge is the epicentre of FR engineering, encompassing locos and carriages. *Blanche* receives some tender loving care outside the running shed. The building behind (to the left) is where heavy overhauls are undertaken.

Early morning preparation can be very atmospheric. Here, *Linda* is being prepared for a day's service.

The 'nameplate' says *Indian Runner*, but this is Hunslet 0-4-0ST *Velinheli* in the yard at Boston Lodge. These temporary nameplates were applied to publicise a potential project to construct a series of new quarry Hunslets although subsequent events resulted in the plan being dropped.

Welsh Pony spent many years on a plinth outside Harbour station. This 12 October 2002 picture shows the loco after it had been moved to Boston Lodge for storage. In 2005 the 1867-built George England loco was painted blue, reflecting a livery applied in the 1930s when *Welsh Pony* worked extensively on the Welsh Highland Railway during the 'rainbow livery' period. Whether it will ever be returned to steam is unknown.

Hunslet 0-4-0ST *Britomart*, privately owned by a consortium,
poses in the sun outside its own private loco shed at Boston Lodge!

Opposite: This picture shows the back of Boston Lodge yard at the seaward end. The carriage shed is on the left, beyond this is the carriage and wagon restoration building. This very unusual location for the 7 October 2000 line-up was chosen for the excellent reason of getting the smokeboxes to face the setting sun. The trouble was, cloud descended and obliterated any chance of evening light! The Hunslet locos had been participating in the Grand Slate Shunt and are (left to right) *Gwynedd, Cloister, Lilla* (at back) and *Alice*.

Inside the works, volunteer Chris Scott gets to work during
an overhaul of *Lilla*, which included lifting the boiler.

The erecting shop is well equipped to undertake repairs and maintenance as demonstrated in the May 1998 picture of *Blanche*, showing the tender lifted clear of the floor.

In the foreground of this May 2002 picture is a power bogie from *David Lloyd George*.
To the right are the frames of Garratt K1 being restored to work on the Welsh Highland Railway.

A long-term project based at Boston Lodge is construction of a reproduction 2-6-2T Lynton & Barnstaple Railway locomotive. Not being a precise replica of an original Manning Wardle, this loco is named *Lyd*. In May 1999 the loco was starting to really take shape following the fitting of the driving wheels, side tanks, smokebox wrapper and chimney. However, there is still much work to be done.

In 1998 a £375,000 Heritage Lottery Fund grant (towards a £500,000 project, the balance of which was provided by the Ffestiniog Railway Society) enabled the restoration of historic FR carriages Nos. 15 and 16, a fleet of slate wagons and, perhaps most important of all, a building in which the work could be undertaken (which, of course, provided the infrastructure for future restoration work). This picture, taken in mid-2000, shows one of the young carriage restoration team members adding the beading to one end of carriage No. 15.

The plaques on the wall in the new carriage and wagon restoration building commemorate its opening on 7 October 1999 following grant assistance from the HLF.

Ffestiniog Railway carriages Nos. 15 and 16 date from 1872 and were the first iron-framed bogie passenger carriages to be built in Britain (for any gauge) and may have been the first such in the world. This picture, taken in mid-2000, shows the exterior work on carriage No. 15 largely complete with the body approaching the point when painting could start.

This replica vehicle under construction, funded by a bequest for the purpose left by the FR's late archivist, Michael Seymour, is arguably the most bizarre narrow gauge vehicle seen on the 2ft gauge in Britain. Charles Easton Spooner's 'Boat' was a four-wheeled private inspection saloon which was hauled up the FR and descended by gravity. The bows reputedly allowed level crossing gates to be pushed open. The original met its demise on February 11 1886 when Spooner, ignoring the basics of single line working, set off without a section staff and collided with an up train. The completed vehicle was 'launched' in October 2005.

This April 2005 picture shows a replica Ashbury carriage under construction at Boston Lodge.

Importantly, the HLF grant to support carriage and wagon restoration included the renovation of a fleet of slate wagons which carried the product which the FR was built to transport in the first place. Two 2-ton wagons are being restored inside the building in the picture, while out in the yard are a number of wagons which have received, or are to due receive, attention.

The magnificent results of the carriage restoration work. This picture shows
carriage No. 16, which was restored to its appearance when last in traffic under
the original FR company (pre-preservation era) in the 1930s; therefore it has
a dark olive-green livery with red oxide ends.

In contrast, carriage No. 15 was returned to 'near as-built' (1872) condition with a 'royal purple' and white livery.

BUILDING A NEW LOCOMOTIVE

The FR constructed locomotives to Fairlie's patent as far back as 1879. The most recent new build was Single-Fairlie *Taliesin*. This is how the locomotive looked in the works at Boston Lodge on 5 May 1997.

Right: The new *Taliesin* was launched in to traffic on 1 May 1999. A few minutes prior to the speeches, Roland Doyle tweaks the nameplate to ensure the loco looks its best. The black livery worn at the time was temporary.

Below: Named after a sixth century Welsh poet, *Taliesin* pulls out of Harbour station on the morning of 1 May 1999 with his first passenger train, a special for invited guests who had assisted the construction project.

By now run-in and given its deep red livery, *Taliesin* is pictured at Minffordd on 5 May 2002.

Blanche wreaths herself with steam as she, and her sister *Linda,* manoeuvre around Harbour station. Almost obscured on the platform road is *Prince* in this 12 October 2002 picture.

DOUBLE-HEADING

George England pairing *Palmerston* and *Prince* do their best to obliterate Porthmadog from view on 1 May 2005 – as if the decidedly indifferent weather was not already doing a pretty fair job!

The sun was considerably more in evidence for this departure by *Earl of Merioneth* and *Mountaineer* on 3 May 2004.

Linda leads *Mountaineer* off the Cob and past Boston Lodge on 3 May 1998.

Double-headed Double-Fairlies – *Earl of Merioneth* and *David Lloyd George*
with a Porthmadog-bound train at Minffordd on 3 May 1998.

MULTIPLE LOCOMOTIVES

Strictly speaking, not a triple-header since they are not hauling a train, but the black-liveried trio of *Lilla*, *Mountaineer* and *Linda* make a fine sight as they reach the Boston Lodge end of the Cob in company on 5 May 2003.

Why limit yourselves to three when four locos can be run together? The cool and slightly damp afternoon on 7 October 2000 undoubtedly contributed to the stupendous volume of steam being exhausted from (left to right) *Palmerston* (FR), *Lilla* (FR), *Gwynedd* (visiting from Bressingham) and *Cloister* (visiting from Kew, owned by the HNGRS) as they come up from the yard at Minffordd to return to Boston Lodge.

Locos working together look terrific, but they look pretty good lined up alongside each other in the sun. This row of FR locos at Porthmadog on the morning of 12 October 2002 comprises (left to right) *Palmerston*, *Taliesin*, *Prince* and *David Lloyd George*.

The ex-Penrhyn ladies, *Blanche* and *Linda*, pose together at Porthmadog
on 7 October 2000 during the FR's Vintage Weekend.

LOCOMOTIVE EXHAUSTS

Exhaust from a locomotive's chimney can be smoke, steam or both – but the effect can be dramatic and/or spectacular. As is fairly obvious, Adrian Shooter's Darjeeling Himalayan Railway B-Class 0-4-0STT No. 19 burns coal as it storms out of Harbour station hauling his matching pair of replica DHR coaches (built by the FR) on 1 May 2005.

In contrast, *Linda* – an oil burner – can happily surround herself in steam as shown while she is prepared at Boston Lodge early on the morning of 23 October 1996.

Continuing with the steamy theme, the morning of 8 October 2000 was magical as locomotives crossed the Cob from Boston Lodge to Harbour station. *Lilla* is arriving with some slate wagons, the locos further away on the Cob are indistinguishable in the strongly back-lit clouds of steam.

This was one of those rare occasions where one cannot resist carrying on shooting pictures, every loco bringing forth a new variation of image. *Linda* is certainly the loco nearest the camera. What is beyond her is hard to say!

This is the distinctive outline of *Blanche* in the series of contre-jour
pictures shot on the early morning of 8 October 2000.

The steamy procession across the Cob on 8 October 2000 was to produce this line-up in the Sunday morning sun at Porthmadog. Left to right are: *Lilla*, *Gwynedd* (from Bressingham), *Alice* (then from Leighton Buzzard, now at Bala Lake) and *Cloister* (Hants Narrow Gauge Railway Society). In addition, between *Lilla* and *Gwynedd* is *Linda*, while on the extreme right, *David Lloyd George* waits to depart with a service train.

Gravity trains down the line tend to come to a stand shortly after the curve opposite Boston Lodge, hence a loco – in this 3 May 2004 instance *Prince* – hauls them onwards to Harbour station, complete with the crew of brakesmen who ride down the line controlling the train.

This picture, deliberately shot almost into the low morning sun to create an interesting lighting effect, shows *David Lloyd George* leaving Porthmadog with a vintage train at 09.30 on 12 October 2002. Behind the Double-Fairlie are 'Bug Boxes' Nos. 5 and 2 while the bogie carriage is bow-side No. 20 – the stock being part of the development of a restored Victorian train on the FR.

The fascinating sight of Adrian Shooter's Darjeeling Himalayan Railway B-Class 0-4-0STT No. 19 hauling the pair of replica DHR coaches setting off across the Cob from Porthmadog on 20 April 2005.

Tiny train, big country. I concede this is a rather extreme interpretation of a train in the landscape as Single-Fairlie *Taliesin* and van No. 10 scoot across the Cob on the evening of 5 May 2003. Intriguingly, to my mind this view shows considerably more water than usual on the landward (far) side of the Cob – a situation rather emphasised by the tide being out, leaving the seaward side almost bereft of water. It is a shade unfortunate that the weather conditions precluded taking this shot in the morning with water up to the Cob on both sides!

As the sign makes clear, *Earl of Merioneth* is approaching Porthmadog Harbour station, the date being 1 August 2000.

Of special interest in this 30 April 2005 picture is the vehicle next to *Prince*. Bogie vans built in the 1870s for the FR became known as 'curly roof vans' due to their unusual roof contour. Constructed when bogie passenger carriages were introduced on the line, the last survivor in original form (No. 3) lay derelict at Harbour station during the FR's closure period and was scrapped (fell apart!) in the mid-1950s. A replica curly roof brake van was built at Boston Lodge, being unveiled in May 2004.

WELSH HIGHLAND RAILWAY (CAERNARFON)

We met NGG16 Garratt No. 138 earlier on Ffestiniog metals. This picture shows it at work on the Welsh Highland Railway (Caernarfon) approaching Hendy crossing between Caernarfon and Dinas on 24 October 1997. Detailing the revival of the WHR is too complex to describe in this volume. Suffice to say, the FR became involved in reviving the WHR, somewhat controversially, in 1987. It officially opened the first section, between Caernarfon and Dinas (not part of the original WHR) on 13 October 1997.

Just yards from the location in the previous picture, the Ffestiniog's *Mountaineer* was photographed while running on the WHR(C) on 28 October 1997.

NGG16 Garratt No. 138 – now repainted in a different shade of green and named *Millennium/Mileniwm* – is pictured at Dinas on 2 June 2002. Dinas was the terminus of the original WHR, the tracks in this view then being a standard gauge line with the narrow gauge on the opposite side of a platform, out of frame to the right.

The FR's next step was to reconstruct the Welsh Highland line proper. The first stage was to rebuild the line between Dinas and Waunfawr. The FR loco *Upnor Castle* is pictured beside the river near Waunfawr in July 2000 as this phase was approaching completion. The author's wife, Carrie, makes another cameo appearance wearing a high visibility jacket in the wagon!

A second ex-South African NGG16 Garratt overhauled by the FR to work on the 'new' line, No. 143, eases out of Dinas yard at 17.45 on Saturday 5 August 2000 and moves on to the original Welsh Highland formation – the first loco to steam on the route since 1936. *Conway Castle* was at the tail of the train, almost hidden behind the four coaches of the historic operation.

More history is made – at about 18.00 on 5 August 2000, No. 143 became the first locomotive to steam into Waunfawr station since 1936. Roland Doyle, who had masterminded reconstruction of the line, walks beside the loco, double-checking clearances as the train moves slowly in to the newly-built platform.

The Dinas to Waunfawr section of the WHR (C) was officially opened on
15 September 2000 and celebrated with the WHR Ffestival 2000 Gala over the weekend
of 16-17 September. The weekend was memorable for fuel shortages, poor weather
forecasts but most especially for the return of Hunslet 2-6-2T *Russell* to the WHR
trackbed for the first time since 1937. *Russell* and NGG16 Garratt No. 138 are
pictured beside the water tower at Caernarfon on 16 September.

Opposite: The forecast of poor weather was all too accurate, the falling rain made
the conditions positively dire when photographing *Russell*, accompanied by the
FR's Alco 2-6-2T *Mountaineer*, at Waunfawr on 17 September 2000!

The next section of the WHR to be opened was between Waunfawr and Rhyd Ddu. Passenger trains returned to Rhyd Ddu in July 2003 with public services between Waunfawr and Rhyd Ddu commencing on 18 August 2003. This view from the cab of NGG16 Garratt No. 143 was taken on 2 May 2004 looking back up the train near Betws Garmon.

The ex-South African NGG16 Garratt No. 143 is pictured later on 2 May 2004 approaching Betws Garmon.

Progressing up the line, No. 143 is pictured later still, framed neatly
between the trees, between Betws Garmon and Plas y Nant.

The Garratt has climbed in to a real mountain landscape now, this picture
being taken on the section just beyond Snowdon Ranger station.

The landscape is ruggedly beautiful on the approach to Rhyd Ddu. If the wind is in the right direction, one can hear Snowdon Mountain Railway locomotives from this location – and on a truly clear day it is possible to see them on the ridge high above!

The final run in to Rhyd Ddu station includes traversing a huge horseshoe curve. No. 143 is pictured easing gently round this feature on its way back to Caernarfon late in the afternoon. The FR is forging ahead with the reconstruction of the line beyond Rhyd Ddu towards Beddgelert and down to Porthmadog, where it will link with the FR at Harbour station.

WELSH HIGHLAND RAILWAY (PORTHMADOG)

A railway has operated since 1980 from a station on the other side of Porthmadog from the FR's Harbour terminus. This short line, belonging to the Welsh Highland Railway Company, operates over land once covered by the standard gauge Beddgelert Siding as far as Pen-y-Mount. This organisation, originally set up as the Welsh Highland Light Railway (1964) Ltd, had always hoped to revive the WHR proper. It also has a priceless asset – the only surviving original Welsh Highland locomotive, Hunslet 2-6-2T *Russell*.

Unsurprisingly, there was much anguish and friction when the FR's interest in reviving the WHR emerged. This is now in the past and a clear statement of how the two companies intended to work together was made when *Russell* visited the WHR (Caernarfon) in September 2000. Reciprocating this, the FR loaned its 0-4-0STT *Palmerston* and two FR carriages to what, for clarity is now known as the WHR (Porthmadog) for the same weekend, 16-17 September. The loco is in the platform of the WHR(P) station at Porthmadog, the train consisting of: FR brake van No 10 (nearest the camera), the WHR(P)'s 'Gladstone Coach' (centre) and FR coach No. 39.

Below: The Welsh Highland Railway (Porthmadog) is particularly orientated towards promoting the heritage aspects of the WHR. Its station building at Pen-y-Mount is a mirror image of the old WHR station building at Nantmoor. The WHR(P) has extended its line from a crossing just to the left of this train, on towards Pont Croesor. This extension will become part of the FR revival of the WHR, linking with the line from Rhyd Ddu from the north and a 'cross town' section which will continue south from Pen-y-Mount through Porthmadog to join the FR at Harbour station.

Left: The 1920s/1930s atmosphere of the WHR(P) is promoted by the dress style of a number of working members, as demonstrated by Ian Jolley. Perhaps he is checking the time of the next train to Rhyd Ddu – or possibly even Blaenau Ffestiniog since the railways will be linked around 2009!